Paleo Ingredients Quiz

J	I	B	A	N	A	N	A	S	U	I	K
A	H	W	C	O	C	O	A	I	U	M	E
R	G	K	V	M	A	N	G	O	R	S	C
A	H	O	N	E	Y	C	H	I	A	L	L
Y	C	U	M	G	B	P	C	Y	N	T	R
Y	L	I	G	W	Y	U	Y	G	K	I	N
Q	I	M	C	H	O	C	O	L	A	T	E
V	J	C	O	C	O	N	U	T	D	S	P
A	Q	F	A	V	O	C	A	D	O	R	S
A	L	M	O	N	D	S	D	P	X	D	W
U	B	L	U	E	B	E	R	R	I	E	S
K	V	M	C	V	Y	A	R	M	F	K	H

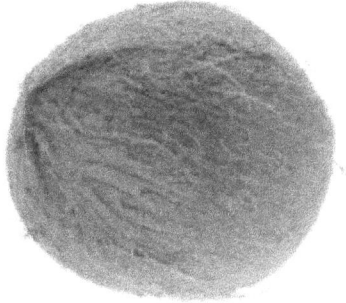

While every precaution has been taken in the preparation of this book, the publisher assumes no responsibility for errors or omissions, or for damages resulting from the use of the information contained herein.

SCRUMPTIOUS PALEO DESSERTS: LOW FAT LOW CHOLESTEROL DESSERT RECIPES FOR A HEALTHY, HAPPY, LEAN & CLEAN EATING LIFESTYLE

First edition. July 25, 2017.

Copyright © 2017 Juliana Baltimoore.

ISBN: 978-1386157205

Written by Juliana Baltimoore.

Introduction

The human diet is a diverse range of flavors and preferences, and has evolved enormously with time. 10,000 years ago cavemen used to hunt for food and devour vegetables and fruits that grew on land. They fished from the sea and hunted wild beasts for their meat. This has been referred to as the Paleolilith era that advocated an organic diet that sufficed to say, was regarded as the diet for optimum health by scientists and doctors. Since, the emergence of agriculture, various toxins and additives have made their way into out diet and have started a chain reaction of several different medical problems like immune system disorders, celiac diseases, and other autoimmune diseases that overtime can cripple human health.

The purpose of this book is not just to take a look at the Paleo diet as a serious health upgrade diet, but it is also to take a peek into the world of Paleo desserts because most people wrongly assume that being on a Paleo diet means you can't have desserts. Let's face it we don't know what desserts were available to the cavemen in their time and it could be really hard to grasp that once you're on a Paleo diet you won't enjoy a cupcake again.

This is the very point with which most scientists and nutrition experts have a beef about with the Paleo diet. They counteract Paleo diet principles with damning views over how due to the vast evolution of human diet, reverting back to a caveman's diet is not something that is altogether doable.

Cavemen never had our technology, or ability to cultivate grains and wheat. In the opinion of modern nutritionists, the caveman diet is as obsolete as a typewriter with the explosion of new technology.

While, they are right to establish that the human tastes and flavors have expanded to new levels that were beyond the scope of cavemen, the Paleo diet isn't really about being a caveman, it's about adapting our diet to meet the organic goodness that sheltered human beings 12000 years ago, and nurtured their bodies with nutrition value that is quite frankly lacking in processed foods and produce of today.

No, Paleo does not mean you go cold turkey on desserts. In fact, the Paleo diet encourages desserts made of organic and fresh products that don't just serve as empty calories, or make you slave to overeating with their high fructose sugar content. Another modern day sucrose conversion that is addictive and present in most foods and drinks, drinks especially, due to its solubility level.

Let's take a look at what the Paleo diet is and what it has to offer.

What Is Paleo & What Will You Learn?

The Paleo diet is one of the most unquestionably interesting diet concepts that have racked up the points in the last few decades. Everyone from celebrities to the general public are adopting it left, right, and center, as the secret of their healthy glow. Health diets and fad diets generally tell you to skimp on desserts, or just altogether forego the bite of a heavenly cream doughnut, but you would be happy to learn that the Paleo diet is one such diet that does not dissuade you from eating those comfort goodies. It in fact, encourages your sweet tooth, but with some adaptive changes that allow for organic ingredients to make up decadent treats that leave your mouth watering for more.

There are several reasons you may have decided to go for Paleo as a lifestyle change, but the need for a dessert treat every now and then remains constant.

So, what is this book about?

1. This book will tell you why Paleo is the craze now?

2. This book will tell you ways in which the Paleo diet will change your lifestyle for the better and turn guilt into guilt free

3. This book will tell you what ingredients to have in your kitchen as a staple for paleo dessert pleasures

4. This book will give you 12 scrumptious paleo desserts (paleo muffins, paleo cupcakes, paleo smoothies & pudding paleo dessert recipes) that you probably desire right now and you will learn how to make these guilt free paleo easy desserts in a quick, easy, and no fail fashion

5. Based on the knowledge of this book you will be empowered and be enabled to discover and explore more and more paleo dessert applications and turn guilt into guilt free pleasures

6. Ultimately, you will be living pleasurable paleo dessert moments free from guilt and this is when you empower yourself to live the paleo lifestyle!

Why Paleo Desserts Work?

You must be wondering why would you want to take a look at Paleo as a serious diet change to improve your lifestyle and health?

There is no shortage of medical journals and newspaper articles, internet bites, and TV infomercials that tell us what is good for the body, what is good for your heart, and what processed food substance will lower your bodies cholesterol. Earlier men and women had longer lives and lesser issues with their health because of natural and organic diets.

This in itself should make you question what are you putting in your bodies these days and what are you feeding your children alike? You may find yourself easily tired at say, age 35, while your father at that age was a tough sport about marathoning through work hours, juggling family, and social activities alike. This is proof that even with evolved diets, eating organic food and eating less processed junk did their bodies actual good.

Now let's enter the Paleo world. As with any other diets, one would be cautious about its overall effect on our body and mind.

Scientific studies, while not a hundred percent accurate, but still, many studies have shown that Paleolilith men/women suffered from none of the hundreds of modern diseases that have been on the rise like an epidemic after the evolution of our diet, and the introductions of agricultural additives and processed food additives that have done the opposite of nurturing our bodies.

But as they all say the proof is in the pudding. Most people who have adapted this lifestyle have nothing but good things to say about this diet. Most importantly, this diet has helped many severely affected patients of different autoimmune diseases achieve restoration of their health almost immediately.

Most of us only hear about gluten in products and how it affects 'some' people badly. If you've heard about gluten free products several times, and don't know why gluten is a common enemy affecting 1 in a 100 cases then, let' talk about gluten.

Gluten is a protein present in all wheat based products and all its cross breeds like rye and barley as well. Today most processed food items apart from wheat products themselves also contain gluten, and it seems that more than some people are badly affecting by the presence of this protein in their foods.

Gluten has been linked to most autoimmune diseases, diarrhea, leaky gut syndrome, intestinal damage, and fatigue to name just a few. The worst part is that most of us don't even know that we may be suffering from any gluten allergies. Many cases of celiac disease remain undiagnosed because sometimes the symptoms are subtle and grow over time, or just don't affect us as severely as it does to some people with diagnosed cases of celiac disease.

Paleo is not just a gluten free diet, it is also a low carb and high fat that encourages the use of some nutritional fat that helps to create energy in a human body. Due to obvious myths that have been fed to us over time through commercials, articles, and scientists we feel afraid of the very mention of 'FAT' in our diet and disregard a high fat diet as complete misnomer.

Fat is not always bad, and carbohydrates only provide energy to that gets burned away immediately. Fats are another macronutrient that give your body the energy to get through the day. Proof of this is the cavemen themselves. They existed on high fat diets that allowed them energy and alertness to hunt and gather for themselves. That can be an intense workout by modern day standards. Out complicated routines of this day is nothing short of intense effort and exertion. A high fat diet will assist in enriching your lifestyle in many ways.

Another issue in our general diet is how our non-Paleo lifestyle affects your blood sugar level and how quickly the blood glucose level rises. All foods have varying glycemic levels (the rate at how quickly your blood sugar level rises with a food) and some make your blood sugar levels increase).

If it's still hard to get a handle on why Paleo should be your diet then let's take a look at the fat free craze that has been on the roll for the last few decades. Fats and saturated fats are both touted as 'evils' that encourage cholesterol and bad heart health, but this is a one sided story. Let's not delve into heavy medical and cellular jargon for it. Keeping it simple, saturated fats aren't all bad fats.

Yes, there are good saturated fats, as well as bad saturated fats. The good fats contribute to good heart health, and don't encourage build up of harmful triglycerides in arteries (what we call clogged arteries are the results of harmful triglycerides build up in our arteries). The macronutrients encouraged in Paleo are all sources of good saturated fats that are productive in increasing heart health and vitality.

Coming to the issue of losing weight with this diet, weight loss can be a seriously frustrating battle if your diet is the one that is hindering your success. Paleo is also know to help slim down those of us who have tried other diets and not found themselves close to shedding those annoying pounds. The low carb, high fat diet that Paleo encourages is also high in its protein quotient. A filling part of the equation that helps keep the individual satiated for longer, and revert to processed foods less.

Once you cut out sugars, high carbs, and gluten out of your diet, you are bound to start dropping pounds. The high protein content also encourages more muscle development and promotes quicker fat burning.

Many organic ingredients in the Paleo diet encourage satiation of appetite and fat burning.

Based on this knowledge we can now move on to look at Paleo from the perspective of being a lifestyle choice that you can make for your own life.

How Paleo Can Change Your Life: The Paleo Lifestyle

The Paleo diet has been called many things, and chief among them is the title of the caveman diet. A name that unwittingly turn some people off right away when they start imagining a bunch of drooling, hulking individuals beating their chests and running through the wild chasing wild beasts. That can be a disconcerting image, but Paleo is known as an all organic diet, and it is also touted as the low carb and high fat diet that can cleanse the body of toxins and additives of the modern processed foods epidemic.

Obesity, heart diseases, and food allergies (like gluten intolerance, celiac disease, diabetes, and other autoimmune disorders) have been on the rise for the last few decades. What hasn't eased these number in the last few years is the rising number of additives, like high fructose corn syrup, sodium, and 'bad' saturated fats in commercially processed cooking oils, and gluten in grains, wheat and all its by products.

We can't put an end to the production of these un-organic foods, but we can protect ourselves from further invasion of harmful diseases that may eventually cripple our body because of the empty calories they represent and their zero nutritional value. Even fortified processed foods that claim to have Vitamins and minerals to make them look more appealing can be deceiving because of the really low percentage of the nutrients present in the foods. And even then you may not be able to absorb those nutrients because of the presence of proteins that can inhibit our body's nutrient absorption by binding themselves to the nutrients and not letting them enter your blood stream.

Let's spell out what the Paleo diet is all about so that there is not confusion about what is shunned in the diet and how you can integrate the Paleo way of eating into your own lifestyle.

Before we do this, however, we must first clarify what ingredients to avoid with the Paleo lifestyle.

Avoid list of Paleo Ingredients

1. **Grains:** Avoid all grains like rice, barley, wheat, rye, quinoa, millet, corn, amaranth, oats, etc. as all of these contain gluten in some degree.

2. **Starchy vegetables:** This means white potatoes. The high starch and high sugar content is not on recommended list in the Paleo diet.

3. **Sugar:** Eliminate sugar from your diet and stick to raw honey and Paleo substitutes such as unsweetened maple syrup (grade B) that avoid raising blood sugar levels exponentially.

4. **Industrial and seed oils:** Avoid vegetable and seed oils like peanut oils, sunflower, canola etc. because they are higher in 'bad' saturated fats, require more processing to become edible and easily go rancid, which creates health issues. Try oils like olive, coconut oil, ghee, and pure grass fed butter.

5. **Legumes:** all kinds of beans whether they be peas, mung beans, broad beans, garbanzo beans, lima beans, and/or peanuts. They have always been touted as healthy proteins, but are also high in carbohydrates and increase insulin release in your body.

6. **Dairy:** Another food source that increases insulin levels in human beings and can contain additives, antibiotics, and growth hormones that can all be harmful to your health.

7. **Sodium:** Use less sodium as it is known to cause bloating, water retention and harmful to human body in higher quantities. Limit your sodium consumption to 1000mg a day. Most processed foods contain sodium (canned beans, premade foods, deli meats, etc.) Try using sea salt instead it's a healthier Paleo option.

Paleo benefits

With this avoid list you must be thinking, how is avoiding any of this stuff make Paleo a good diet to be on? What are its benefits? After all if I'm giving up my pizza dough, I need to know it's got to be for some worthwhile reason. No way is any diet worth giving a try if you're going to be off the conventional pizza's made of gluten flour and fizzy drinks that are full of high fructose corn syrup.

Let's talk about some Paleo benefits that are sure to peak your interest.

1. Say goodbye to being 'hangry'. This is a combination of being both hungry and angry. Being on a high fat and low carbohydrate diet helps you stay satiated for longer. Some people experience rapid drop in their blood sugar, which is followed by hunger and irritability. This is called hypoglycemia, but the Paleo diet will help with satiety and you will find yourself eating less than with other diets.

2. Experience sustained weight loss. Because of Paleo's food principles, you are consuming natural, organic, process free foods that help in controlling your weight. Processed carbs, sugar, and excess sodium are chief causes of weight gain. In a Paleo diet, once you get rid of foods that are discouraged by Paleo, you will notice a dramatic improvement in your weight and your ability to sustain that weight loss. Many studies have proved that things like high fructose corn syrup (a sweetener present in many processed food items) can be addictive. The HFCS is serving as empty calories itself, and your digestive system digests fructose in a different way from sucrose, but this is not the only cause of weight gain. HFCS is known to be addictive and when you drink one too many cans of some fizzy drink, you are bound to put on pounds.

3. No more bloating and being gassy all the time. You may have noticed that as you get older, eating certain foods causes your body to bloat and you are always gassy at night. This is common if you consume sodium more than 1000mg a day. With Paleo, the use of sodium and salt is discouraged because of its side effects that cause you to bloat, become gassy, and also unable to burn fat if you are trying to lose weight.

4. Healthy fats like omega 3 are encouraged in the Paleo diet. The nutritional value of omega 3 has always been immense, but with this diet you intake of this fatty acid increases to exponential levels. Consuming omega 3 regularly benefits your hearth, helps you burn fat quicker, helps you control autoimmune diseases like diabetes, and promotes positive brain development and a much healthier immune system.

5. Eating un-processed food is the ultimate benefit. This is something that cannot be overlooked about being on a Paleo diet. This diet encourages you to eat natural, organic food, and tells you to avoid harmful processed foods that are full of negative additives, toxins, antibiotics, and growth hormones that are bad for your health anyway. Above all it has a good balance of macronutrient (protein, carbohydrates, and fats) and their appropriate ratios, which should not only nourish and give you exceptional overall health, but also give you mental clarity and a generally better mood.

6. You will be in optimum health because you will be consuming many nutrients and Vitamins that contribute to giving you good energy for the day, strengthen your immune system and the good fats in a Paleo diet will help with good health of arteries, maintain good skin and healthy brain function.

7. When you are on a Paleo diet the fats, and oils you use will not be harmful to your body because the oils used on a Paleo diet tend to be largely stable and don't go rancid like other commercial vegetable and seed oils that go rancid quickly, which brings about a toxicity to the oil that can be damaging to your body and promote negative heart health.

8. Eating habits really affect your sleep. People on Paleo diet, have a better overall health, this means better gut health, less bloating, less gassiness, water retention and better sleeping patterns. You will sleep better when you aren't troubled by an upset stomach, or the feeling of being bloated.

While, it may be a bit easier to give up savory foods and snacks, it can be much harder and more painful to let go off everyday desserts like muffins, cakes, cookies, and ice cream. There's a whole culture of comfort built around these desserts. Gossiping friends, lovers on a romantic dinner, or a family night of movies and ice cream, how can you make the transition to a better lifestyle easier without sugar, butter, and flour?

Let's take a peek into the world of guilt free Paleo desserts that are healthy but very tasty and scrumptious at the same time. Once you get the idea that healthy and delicious can work in combination, you will be hooked on the Paleo lifestyle forever.

Sneak Peek Into The World Of Paleo Desserts

Paleo desserts can be a wondrous world of treats and tastes, if you use the right Paleo ingredients and have yummy recipes on hand to try them. It can be hard to know where to get started when you don't have an idea about Paleo ingredients. After all, what can a cupcake be without milk and sugar? What can a chocolate pudding be without actual chocolate in it? And how can a cheese cake be creamy without a giant helping of cream cheese?

Seems depressing when you think all the flavors you may be missing out on because you're removing all wheat, sugars, and dairy products from your diet. Fear not! There are Paleo substitutes for all those ingredients and more. This chapter will shine a light on all those ingredients, and give you an idea of how to use them compared to conventional ingredients used for desserts.

Grain free flours

The key to most desserts is good quality flour. The flour can make or break a cupcake. So, what does Paleo have to offer the texture aficionados of desserts?

Almond flour:

This is made from finely ground almonds, and gives grainier texture to desserts, but it can be substituted with other flours in a 1:1 ratio. It however, doesn't contain gluten, so while that is good for your health, you may find that it does not provide a dessert with the same elasticity and hold that gluten does with the conventional flours. Not to worry though, you can use this flour for cookies and bakes that need a grainier texture, or substitute slightly with some other Paleo flour for desired texture.

Tips:

1. Keep in mind also that the finer the almond flour is the better a baked dessert will turn out.

2. Keep in mind that nut flour can easily brown, so, keep the heat lower than usual and bake your dessert for longer to compensate for a lower temperature.

3. Keep the almond flour refrigerated, or even frozen and it will last longer.

2. Coconut flour: This is another prized Paleo flour that is approved for dessert making and give batters and desserts a good texture. You can expect a lighter and airier cupcake with this flour. However, coconut flour cannot be substitutes at a 1:1 ratio with other flours because of the rate at which it absorbs liquid. You can substitute about ¼ cups of coconut flour with 1 cup of any other nut based, or grain based flour. With about ½ a cup coconut use 5 eggs and ½ a cup of coconut milk to compensate for the absorbent nature of coconut flour.

Tips:

1. Try adding mashed fruit for moisture in the baking.
2. Store your coconut flour at room temperature.
3. Sift your flour before using it, as it tends to be clumpy.

Fats and oil

Choosing a Paleo fat that will both compliment a dessert and not contribute to bad cholesterol isn't hard when it comes to Paleo. Many healthy examples are available that both do justice to a scrumptious dessert recipe and also provide good health benefits.

- Use coconut oil and butter in desserts, this is a stable oil at high temperatures and works well in recipes which call for a vegetable oil, or shortening. Earlier concerns of the amount of saturated fats in coconut oil have been outweighed by the benefits of this oil. This oil increases metabolic rate and also contributes positively to the immune system.

- Use almond butter, or any other nut butter in your desserts, they add decadence and are creamy and make your baking smell amazing.

- Use grass fed butter or ghee in your desserts. Additive and antibiotic free butter and ghee are high in good saturated fats.

Dairy:

Use coconut milk, or almond milk. Both work well in most of the dessert recipes and provide great flavor. Coconut milk gives great coconut cream frosting that tastes amazing when whipped.

Sweeteners:

There are many Paleo approved sweeteners like medjool dates, grade B maple syrup, and honey that have made the list and can be substituted for sugar in dessert recipes. Raw honey is the best of the list and considered closely approved by the Paleo diet as an organic ingredient that is good for human body and does not exponentially increase blood sugar levels in your body. Dates are great for incorporating sweetness in both baked goods and pudding and ice creams. They provide an amazing amount of sweetness, and are still good for your health.

Chocolate:

Chocolate cake without cocoa?, chocolate pudding without chocolate? No way! Don't worry, the Paleo diet allows for unsweetened cocoa powder, or raw version of it called cacao powder.

Use dark chocolate with 70% cocoa content, or 85% cocoa content, or use unsweetened dark chocolate.

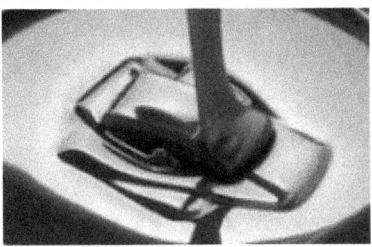

Paleo Food List

Target the crops that are in season so as to get the very best costs and nutrient content. Stock up on what's on sale many plants can be frozen for subsequent use.

Great decisions include: greens, spinach, broccoli, cauliflower, zucchini, asparagus, cabbage, brussels sprouts, onions, fresh herbs, garlic, sweet potatoes (for post workout meals), tomatoes, mushrooms, aubergine, avocado and bell peppers.

If you have autoimmune issues make sure to avoid nightshades.

Fit fruit into your diet basically in the post workout period.

If selecting farm raised meat go for the leanest cut and if grass fed the fat is very good.

Sirloin, tenderloin, strip steaks and flank are the leanest decisions. Game birds When selecting game birds the thigh portions and the breast portions will provide the most protein and from a food to money proportion are the best chance.

Salmon, tuna and other greasy fish are the very best choices due to their high Omega-3 trans-acid content.

Omega 3 fortified eggs from free range chickens are the best choice.

Many times here's where folks get in difficulty.

Walnut oils and avocado are also excellent on salads.

Coconut milk (the kind in a can with no sugar added), in post workout smoothies, and as an alternative choice to creamer if you are a coffee drinker.

Nuts and specifically nut butters are also great to have around for fast nibbles and in a pinch.

Macadamia nuts and walnuts are the top choices and walnut butter is just wonderful .

When selecting nut butters ensure there aren't any added ingredients.

Paleo & Fiber?

There are some questions that we find come up all the time when we are talking about Paleo. People who are looking make the transit into the paleo lifestyle are always asking us questions related to fiber.

For example, does a Paleo lifestyle provide me with enough fiber because with Paleo there are no grains allowed? People are asking things about whole grains and fiber because they know that these foods do fight cholesterol.

People are confused about the fact that they need a certain amount of fiber into their system in order to stay healthy.

We always get the questions what are the best sources of fiber with the Paleo lifestyle.

People are also not clear about if fiber helps them keep themselves full in order to lose weight when they are on a diet.

All these questions and concerns show how people are unclear and confused about Paleo and fiber and that is the reason why we are dedicating one whole chapter to this topic because it is important to clear up the confusion before we get any further into the main content.

The best way you can start to fix your digestive tract and stomach health is by getting rid of poisonous foods for good :
- Cereal grains are bad
- Omega 6 economic seed oils (things like corn, safflower, cottonseed, soybean, and the like) are bad
- Processed soy (like soya milk, soy flour and soy protein for example) is bad

Many people have diverse food sensitivities, with some of the more common perpetrators being dairy and gluten.

Removing a number of these items, and including fermentable foods like kefir, kimchi and sauerkraut may do the job in restoring some healthy tummy bacteria.

You may also help to boost your health by including the right kinds and amounts of fiber. The Institute of Medication commends around thirty eight grams of fiber for men, and twenty-five grams for girls roughly a day.

Though it isn't wholly important to hit these numbers, a paleo approach to eating will get you extremely close if it does not surpass them. A one thousand calorie portion of fruit and veg will offer you approximately 2 to 7 times the quantity of fiber than whole grains would. And , the majority of this fiber is from soluble sources which are far more favorable in the sense that they feed the healthful bacteria in your stomach.

Soluble fiber ferments in the tummy, and turns into short chain trans-acids that, in turn, help to grow, and feed healthy bacteria. By including more green leafy vegetables, root veg, and tubers like carrots and sweet potato, as well as low sugar fruits like berries, you can add more fiber to your diet, and improve stomach health, but improve mineral and vitamin uptake and assimilation.

Due to phytates and gluten found in foods like beans and numerous wheat-based products, many minerals and vitamins like calcium, iron, and zinc can go unabsorbed. The plants and occasional fruits on a paleo diet supply more than sufficient fiber to your body.

In fact cups of cooked broccoli would provide you with 7 grams of fiber and only thirty calories, while it would probably take 2 bits of "whole grain" that equal 120 calories to supply the same quantity of fiber.

Constipation and regular elimination

If staying regular with your guts is an important concern, we suggest first looking at your water consumption. Dehydration or an absence of water is mostly to blame for a poor digestion. It's also possible the grains, dairy, and legumes you were dependent on eating caused leaky tummy.

The most effective way to deal with this is by removing food most dangerous to the bowel like commercial seed oils, grains, dairy, and legumes, and by permitting the good bacteria and abdominal flora to reset themselves, and mend the tummy lining. 75 percent of stool is dry weight or dead bacteria, suggesting that fiber isn't required for bulk and elimination.

It can certainly help, but isn't a duty. So long as your body maintains healthy stomach flora, and you steer clear of food that body doesn't endure well, and high fructose foods like honey, soda, agave, breakfast bars and cereals as well as processed junk, you will be able to prevent bowel problems, swelling and gas.

Fiber supplementation

Many supposed health specialists advocate taking extra fiber products to help with weight management, the lowering of cholesterol, and trots. The issue with this is that your body, or, more particularly, your colonic tract, can become hooked on these products, and need more of them. If you're following a lower carbohydrate diet, and are fighting with the constancy of your stools and cholesterol, first try slowly pushing up your water consumption by roughly 8 oz every day. Then think of adding in more starchy and fermentable foods like sweet potatoes and carrots. Eventually , if those things don't help, or if you have blood sugar issues, and can not include starchy carbs, give consideration to adding in a soluble fiber supplement like Organic Acacia Fiber, or a prebiotic like Klaire Laboratories Biotagen. In every case, begin reinforcement with a low dose, and steadily increase weekly or bi-weekly.

Fiber and cholesterol

Fiber and cholesterol This could be the number one thing that frustrates me more than the rest in the world of nourishment.

We wish to kick the people that started this rumor.

We just wish to touch on a pair things here. Cholesterol isn't bad. Your body real wants it so as to operate capably. Cholesterol is employed to make cell surfaces, which are used to help each single cell in your body move, and engage with the other cells. The cholesterol you eat has just about nothing to do with the cholesterol in your blood. You eat cholesterol, and create your very own cholesterol each day.

Approximately 25 percent of your daily cholesterol is from the food that you eat, and the other 75 percent is basically manufactured by your body. The majority of the cholesterol you eat and produce each day lives in your cell surfaces. It's actually serving a purpose.

Cholesterol in your blood does not imply cholesterol in your arteries. When you get your cholesterol checked, what's measured is the quantity of cholesterol in the blood. The reality is that there is not any way of knowing if that cholesterol is going to finish up in your arteries or not.

Almost all of the cholesterol you eat is pooped out. There's no other way to put it truly. Most cholesterol you eat isn't soaked up - it leaves the body in your stool. Real reasons behind coronary disease are deep set in swelling. This is due generally to the overconsumption of Omega-6 fats from grains, plant oils, and grain-fed animals. One way you may help to combat this is by getting rid of these foods from your diet, and including fitter Omega 3 fats from wild-caught salmon, bolstering with fish oil, and eating more grass-fed meat and lamb.

Rather than counting up fiber grams, mixing up high fibre supplement shakes, taking in nonsensical amounts of grains or legumes, or hunting for fake foods with added fiber, instead get back to eating real food.

Stress green leafy plants, lower sugar fruits like berries, and fermentable starchy carbohydrates like sweet potatoes and carrots, increase that water consumption, get routine exercise, and, for Pete's sake, get your rest, and practice correct stress-relieving systems like meditation. Not merely will that keep you regular - it will keep you healthy, content, and fit too.

Before You Get Started Set Your Goal Straight

The book is written for beginners and for advanced users of the Paleo lifestyle.

We recommend to beginners to get right through the recipes and set yourself a goal. Choose one recipe and just get started with it. Just give it a chance and go through your own experience and see how changing food ingredients is going to affect your health and happiness in general.

If you are an advanced student of the Paleo lifestyle, you will probably want to add more of the Paleo lifestyle to what you are already doing with it and probably you picked up this book to add more Paleo recipes to your collection. Well, you are going to be surprised because this book only contains the most exclusive and the most delicious Paleo dessert recipes for Paleo gourmets.

No matter if you already are enjoying the Paleo lifestyle or if you are new to it, this book is for everybody who is conscious about what is going on with the unhealthy food industry and who wants to change one's lifestyle into a healthy and happy lifestyle that the Paleo way of thinking is able to offer anybody who is willing to change some eating habits.

You will soon see that it is not hard to make these lifestyle changes, but if you do you will get way more out of it than you put into it. You will also get a better understanding and feel for the Paleo lifestyle because Paleo is not just a diet or a diet plan that must be adhered like a diet that is not enjoyable to go through. Paleo is a way of thinking, a philosophy and a lifestyle because if you accept the rules and the paleo ingredients, you can integrate Paleo into everything that you are doing with food.

You will understand that there is no limit like it is the case with a diet because you can apply the Paleo lifestyle to every meal or treat that you desire to enjoy! If you understand this concept, you will be able to get the maximum out of Paleo. Once you are able to turn your life into the Paleo lifestyle and experience the Paleo lifestyle to the fullest, you will see the true power of it.

If you are not used to the Paleo lifestyle yet, make sure to read through the book in a very open and unbiased way. Make sure to read it without being ignorant to new things that you will learn and that might not fit into your model or into what you have been learning about food and health until today.

Before you get started with something new like this make sure to free yourself from preconceived notion and look at everything with a pair of fresh eyes so that you can maximize your understanding.

We are sure you get the idea, but it is important to get your mindset and goal straight before getting started with something new like this.

Now that you are getting the point, let's actually hop into the fun part of the book and get to the gourmet class Paleo desserts that we all desire eating so joyfully after a nice meal or just as a special treat during our busy days.

Let's get started with the scrumptious gourmet Paleo dessert recipes. This is where the fun begins because you are about to learn how to turn guilt into guilt free pleasures!

Paleo Muffin Recipes

Creamy Coconut Macadamia Paleo Muffins With Raw White Chocolate Frosting

Ingredients (makes 8 muffins)
   Muffins

   1) 4 eggs
   2) 2 cups almond meal
   3) 2 tsp baking powder
   4) 1/2 cup macadamia nuts
   5) 1/2 cup coconut oil (melted)
   6) 1/3 cup coconut cream
   7) 1 tsp vanilla extract

Raw white chocolate frosting

   1) 1 cup raw cashews
   2) 1 tbsp raw honey
   3) ½ cup cacao butter (small pieces shaved)
   4) 1 tsp lemon juice
   5) 1 tsp almond extract
   6) 4 tbsp coconut milk

Directions

   1) Pre-heat your oven to 350 degrees.

Line cookie sheets with 8 baking cups or use your favorite reusable muffin molds

   3) In a bowl combine the baking powder, almond meal.

   4) In another bowl combine the coconut oil, cream, and vanilla extract. Add eggs one at time until properly combined.

   5) Add the wet mixture to the dry mixture, mixing in the macadamia nuts.

   6) Scoop into muffin cups, baking them for 15 minutes.

Raw white chocolate frosting

1) Except for the coconut milk add all the ingredients to a food processor and process until creamy and then add the coconut milk 1 tablespoon at a time to the frosting until you reach the desired consistency.

Almond Butter & Chocolate Banana Protein Paleo Muffins with Toasted Whipped Coconut Cream

Ingredients (makes 6 muffins)
Muffins

1. ½ cup gluten free oats
2. 2 scoops chocolate protein powder
3. ¼ tsp baking powder

4. ¼ tsp baking soda
5. 2 egg whites
6. 1 ripe banana
7. 2 tbsp stevia
8. ½ cup almond butter
9. 2 tbsp almond butter

Frosting

1. 2 cans of coconut milk (refrigerated)
2. 1 ½ tsp vanilla extract
3. 1 ½ tbsp maple syrup (unsweetened)
4. ½ cup Shredded unsweetened coconut

Directions
Muffins

1. Pre-heat your oven to 350 degrees.

2. Whisk together in a bowl the oats, baking powder, soda, stevia, and soda.

3. In a separate bowl mash the banana and whisk into it the egg whites, almond butter and milk.

4. Now combine the wet ingredients with the dry ones.

5. Scoop into muffin pre-greased, or lined muffin cups ¾ of the way full and bake the muffins for 23 minutes. If you like to push the easy baking button just use the time & tear saving reusable muffin molds

Frosting

1. Make the whipped coconut cream by in a mixer with the cream on the top of the coconut milk can, vanilla extract, and maple syrup. Just make sure you don't shake, or turn the coconut milk can upside down after refrigerating the can.

2. To toast the shredded coconut bake it in the oven for 20 minutes at 300 degrees.

Paleo Cupcake Recipes

Gluten Free Paleo Coconut Cupcakes with Coconut Whipped Cream Frosting

SCRUMPTIOUS PALEO DESSERTS: LOW FAT LOW CHOLESTEROL DESSERT RECIPES FOR A HEALTHY, HAPPY, LEAN & CLEAN EATING LIFESTYLE

Ingredients (makes 12 cupcakes)
Cupcakes

1. 3 eggs
2. 2 ripe banana (mashed)
3. 4 tbsp coconut milk
4. ½ cup coconut flour
5. 2 tbsp cup raw honey
6. 1 tsp baking powder
7. ¼ tsp baking soda
8. 1 tsp vanilla extract
9. ½ cup macadamia nuts (chopped)

Frosting

1. ¼ cup tahini
2. 3 oz cocoa butter
3. 1 tsp vanilla extract
4. 1 tsp arrowroot powder
5. ¼ cup honey
6. ¼ cup butter (grass-fed)

Directions
Cupcakes

1. Pre-heat your oven to 350 degrees

2. Mix together in a bowl, coconut flour, almond flour, baking soda, baking powder, vanilla extract, and eggs.

3. Melt the coconut oil together with honey until well combined.

4. Slowly add the honey and oil mixture to the earlier mixture you made. Mix in the macadamia nuts.

5. Pour into muffin cups before placing in oven and baking for 25 minutes.

6. Now cool them completely before frosting.

Frosting

1. Melt the cocoa butter over a double boiler and add honey until all well combined.

2. Add rest of the ingredients and mix together until well incorporated.

3. Let the mixture cool at room temperature and whisk using a hand mixer until the mixture reaches a frosting consistency.

Bittersweet Chocolate Mango Coconut Paleo Cupcakes with Raw Coffee Roast Frosting

Ingredients (makes 8 cupcakes)

Cupcakes

1. 2 cans coconut milk
2. 4 eggs
3. 40g cacao powder, or unsweetened cocoa powder
4. 80g coconut palm sugar
5. 45g coconut flour
6. 125g almond meal
7. ½ tsp baking soda
8. 125 ml ripe mango pulp

Frosting

1. 2 avocados (peeled, pitted)
2. ½ cup strong brewed coffee
3. ½ cup honey

4. 2 tbsp coconut oil (solid form)
5. 1 tsp vanilla extract
6. ½ tsp salt

Directions
Cupcakes

1. Whisk the eggs together with coconut sugar, in a bowl, until the sugar is dissolved.

2. Now sift the coconut flour, cocoa powder, baking soda, baking powder and almond meal together, adding half of the sifted mixture to the egg and sugar mixture.

3. Whisk until smooth. Add the mango to the batter and slowly add rest of the dry mixture to this batter and beat in the mixer until, it's well incorporated.

4. Pour the batter into the pre lined and greased muffin tin molds and place in the oven for about 20 minutes. If you like to push the easy baking button just use the time & tear saving reusable muffin molds

Frosting

1. Blend all the ingredients together in a mixer, until smooth and you have the desired consistency for your frosting.

Paleo Pudding Recipes

Dark Paleo Chocolate Chia Coconut Paleo Pudding with Decadent Coconut Pecan Paleo Topping

Ingredients (makes 4 muffins)
   Pudding

1. 1000g Dark chocolate (with 85% cocoa, chopped)
2. 2 tbsp cocoa powder
3. 12 tbsp chia seeds
4. 3 tsp vanilla extract

5. 2 cans of coconut milk

Topping

1. ¼ cup pecans (chopped)
2. ½ cup shredded coconut
3. 1 tbsp coconut oil
4. 2 tbsp almond butter
5. 2 tbsp honey
6. 1 tbsp vanilla extract

Directions
Pudding

1. Combine dark chocolate, cocoa powder and coconut milk in a saucepan over medium heat, completely melting the chocolate.

2. Stir in the chia seeds after turning the heat off and sit continuously otherwise the chia seeds will stick to the bottom.

3. Let the chia seeds thicken up the mixture before spooning into small serving bowls.

4. Refrigerate the bowls for one hour, until the pudding is really thick,

Topping

1. Melt coconut oil over medium heat, stir in the honey, vanilla extract, and the almond butter.

2. When combined, pour over pecans and the shredded coconut and stir with a fork until crumbly.

Blueberry Paleo Pudding with Dried Apricots with White Cream Topping

Ingredients
Pudding

1. 2 cups frozen blueberries
2. ⅔ cup almond milk
3. 5 large dates (soaked in hot water)
4. ½ of a frozen banana
5. ½ cup chia seeds (soaked)
6. ½ cup dried apricots (chopped roughly)

Topping

1. 1 can of coconut milk (refrigerated)
2. 1 tsp vanilla extract
3. 1 tbsp maple syrup (unsweetened)

Directions
Pudding

1. Add the blueberries, milk, dates, banana and chia seeds to food processor and pulse until well blended.

2. Add the dried apricots and pulse one more just to incorporate well.

Topping

1. Make the whipped coconut cream by in a mixer with the cream on the top of the coconut milk can, vanilla extract, and maple syrup. Just make sure you don't shake, or turn the coconut milk can upside down after refrigerating the can.

2. Serve putting with a spoon of coconut cream on top and some shredded, unsweetened coconut.

Dark & Intense High Protein Chocolate Paleo Pudding with Coconut Whip Cream

Ingredients (2 servings)
  Pudding

1. ¼ cup coconut milk
2. ½ ripe avocado
3. 1 egg
4. 2 ½ tbsp cacao powder
5. 1 tbsp instant coffee
6. Pinch of salt
7. 1 scoop vanilla whey protein powder
8. A handful of hazelnuts

Topping

1. 1 can coconut milk
2. 1 tsp vanilla extract
3. 1 ½ tbsp honey

Directions
Pudding

1. Add the egg, coconut milk, and avocado to the food processor blending very well, until thick and creamy.

2. Now add in the cacao powder, instant coffee, salt, and protein powder until all creamy and well combined.

3. Now add the hazelnuts, giving a good spin, which incorporated them into the pudding well.

4. Pours into dessert cups and refrigerate before serving.

5. Garnish with some shredded unsweetened coconut for more crunch.

Topping

1. Whip the coconut cream (remove the cream from the top of the coconut milk without shaking it after you have refrigerated it.) with the vanilla extract, and honey until nice and whipped to soft peaks.

Paleo Smoothie Recipes

Creamy Paleo Coconut Macadamia Coffee Smoothie

Ingredients (makes 1 serving)

1. ½ cup coffee (cold)
2. ¾ cup coconut milk
3. ½ cup avocado
4. ¼ cup macadamia nuts
5. ¼ cup ice
6. 2-3 medjool dates

Directions:

1. Put all the ingredients in a blender and blend until smooth.

Scrumptious Cake Batter Paleo Smoothie

Ingredients (Makes 1 serving)

1. 1 tbsp macadamia nut butter
2. 2 medjool dates
3. 1 cup almond milk
4. 1 frozen banana
5. ½ tsp vanilla extract
6. 1 scoop vanilla protein powder

Directions:

1. Put all the ingredients in a blender and blend until smooth.

Creamy Paleo Coconut Macadamia Coffee Smoothie

Ingredients (1 serving)
 1. Coconut milk - 3/4 cup
 2. Cold coffee - 1/2 cup
 3. Avocado - 1/4 cup
 4. Macadamia nuts - 1/4 cup
 5. Ice - 1/4 cup
 6. Stevia - 2 scoops.

Directions

1. Add all the recipes into the blender and blend until a smooth consistency is attained. Garnish it with a few macadamia nuts and almond flakes for an added texture.

This smoothie is also a great idea as a low carb breakfast recipe as it uses coconut milk instead of full fat milk and uses stevia which is a low calorie substitute for sugar .Hence this is also a dairy free and gluten free recipe.

Paleo Ice Cream Recipes

Paleo Butter Pecan Salted Caramel Paleo Ice Cream

Ingredients
   Ice cream (makes 1 quart ice cream)

   1. 1 large egg
   2. 2 tbsp raw honey
   3. 1 ½ tsp vanilla extract
   4. 2 tbsp arrowroot powder
   5. Pinch of salt

6. 1 tbsp almond butter

Caramel sauce (1/3 cup caramel sauce)

1. 1 tsp vanilla extract
2. ¼ cup coconut palm sugar
3. 2 tbsp water
4. ½ cup coconut milk
5. Pinch of salt

Directions
Ice cream

1. Combine the arrowroot powder, milk, egg, honey, and salt in a low heat saucepan. Bring the mixture gently to a boil.

2. Cool for 5 minutes and then add the vanilla.

3. Now refrigerate the mixture overnight.

4. Take the pecans and fry them in butter until they are golden and then add them to the frozen ice cream mixture.

5. Churn the mixture in an ice cream maker swirling in the caramel sauce with a butter knife.

Caramel sauce

1. Boil the coconut palm sugar and water gently, stirring constantly.

2. Now add the milk, salt, and vanilla extract cooking it medium heat for 10 minutes, until the mixtures thicken and becomes a darker color.

Lavender Blueberry Jam Paleo Ice Cream with Organic Lemon Curd

Ingredients (makes 3-4 servings)
Blueberry jam

1. ¼ cup raw honey
2. 1 tsp vanilla extract
3. 1 tbsp lavender buds (finely ground)
4. 1 cup blue berries

Ice cream

1. 1 can coconut milk
2. 1 tsp almond extract
3. 1/3 cup raw honey

Lemon curd

1. 6 tbsp lemon juice
2. Zest of 1 lemon
3. 1 tsp raw honey
4. 2 eggs

Directions

1. Add the blueberries and honey to a saucepan on medium heat.

2. Let the blueberries burst and reduce to thickened, jam like consistency.

3. Now add the salt, lavender, and the vanilla mixing properly.

4. Once you notice that the blueberries are completely broken down, put it aside and let it cool.

5. Heat lemon juice, honey, and lemon zest in a sauce pan, simmering for 2 minutes. Now slowly add eggs and keep whisking in a vigorous manner. Remove from heat and allow cooling.

6. Now whisk coconut milk, honey, and the almond extract.

7. Add the mixture to the ice cream churning machine and churn until thick. When it is thick add the blue berry jam and the lemon curd alternating between both little by little until all incorporated and the ice cream has formed.

Conclusion

Finding the right kind of dessert that appeases your taste buds should not be a problem with the decadent examples of desserts that can be whipped up with Paleo ingredients. Not only are they fresh, but these recipes are quick.

This book was meant to give you a peek into the world of Paleo desserts, and these twelve recipes are by no means the complete look at the versatility of Paleo ingredients. Paleo might be somewhat limited approved ingredients, but it is by no means limited in providing taste to your favorite desserts.

Making the change over to a Paleo way of life can be a big change and can take some getting just to, but the health benefits are unrivaled and far greater than not accepting the challenge and putting your health before processed food cravings.

The 'craze' of Paleo as you will discover with your increased knowledge of the Paleo diet is not just a craze, or a fad diet that will eventually melt away into the unknown depths of forgotten failed diet fads. Paleo is here to stay and steadily rising in popularity. What you can do to get a better feel of what you are getting into is gain as much knowledge of the ingredients and Paleo concepts that bring about that wonderful change in your life that everyone else who has been getting positive results from the Paleo lifestyle has been experiencing.

Hopefully by now you do understand the true significance and meaning of the Paleo lifestyle and hopefully you can see what the Paleo lifestyle can do for your own health and happiness.

As mentioned before, Paleo is not a diet. A diet has limits, but the Paleo way of thinking can be adapted to everything related to food, recipes, baking and cooking that your mind desires.

Be as creative with it as you like, but just respect the Paleo rules that you can refer back to in the beginning of this book.

We chose to demonstrate Paleo with dessert recipes so that you do understand this powerful lifestyle that you can create for yourself. Usually, dessert recipes are associated by society with guilt and shame, but at the same time with pleasure. To show you the power of Paleo we chose the toughest type of food that is desserts in order to show you how Paleo can even be applied to sugar and guilt loaded desserts.

As you got started reading the book, you probably thought guilt free desserts no way and it looked impossible and suspicious to you to turn desirable desserts that are associated with guilt into something guilt free.

This book is going to enables you to figure out the problem how to turn any desired food type like desserts into a pleasure that is guilt free because it respects the rules of the Paleo lifestyle.

Once you have figured out this problem you are in the zone, at least mentally, so we congratulate you on reading through the book and getting the knowledge that you need in order to make this lifestyle change a successful one.

Make sure to go to the next step and that is taking action. Make sure to have a clear goal in mind and get started with one or two recipes and explore more from there.

Now you have learned that Paleo is not something like a diet that comes with limits, but you have been able to see with your very onw eyes how even desserts that we desire and love eating but that we have been conditioned not to eat so much because they are bad for us can be turned into a an exciting new experience that is far away from feeling guilty about something like desserts.

We encourage you to explore this lifestyle further on your own and have fun to find out many other guilt free Paleo recipe applications for yourself. This knowledge empowers you to explore new levels and dimensions of eating that you have never thought possible before.

Do not let anybody tell you that this is not the way to go. Do not become discouraged if little things do not turn out right once in a while. Keep trying until you reach your goal. Once you are able to see it and apply it to your daily meal plan, you will never want to go back to your past eating habits.

Once you are able to apply Paleo to all your food choices, you will feel the magical power of Paleo and that is when you are living the Paleo Lifestyle!

Extra Bonuses

To make your Paleo lifestyle even more exciting we have included some additional bonuses below for you to check out. These bonuses are complementary to the book and are meant to add some more valuable items that you might find helpful as you are going through your Paleo exploring phase.

They are just there to give some additional guidance on things like healthy eating and healthy food ingredients, inspirational moments, dessert making and baking supply resources that might come in handy as you are making these wonderful paleo dessert recipes, as well as some other helpful ideas that relate to decorating, storing and serving desserts.

These are some optional reads and are not necessary at all because by now you have enough knowledge about Paleo desserts and most importantly you know how to turn a guilt and sugar loaded dessert into a guilt free pleasure because you are empowered by a system that you can apply whenever and wherever you like.

We have even included our secret couponing method for you to double your baking fun.

Also make sure to check out our new book releases that are going to be part of our Oh So Scrumptious Paleo series that we will be continuing.

We will be adding our new book releases to the More Information chapter of this book as soon as they become available.

You can also check out our Facebook page where we announce new releases, check the marketplace on a regular basis for our upcoming books, or get access to our free Paleo lifestyle membership where you will get even more Paleo lifestyle pleasures, including a regular prize giveaway of "Favorite Oprah" Paleo things and baking supplies.

Inside you will receive many delightful goodies that will help you with your Paleo lifestyle in a big way.

To get to the links in order to get access to our Paleo Pleasures and to connect with us, please check out the More Information section below.

Paleo Ingredients Quiz

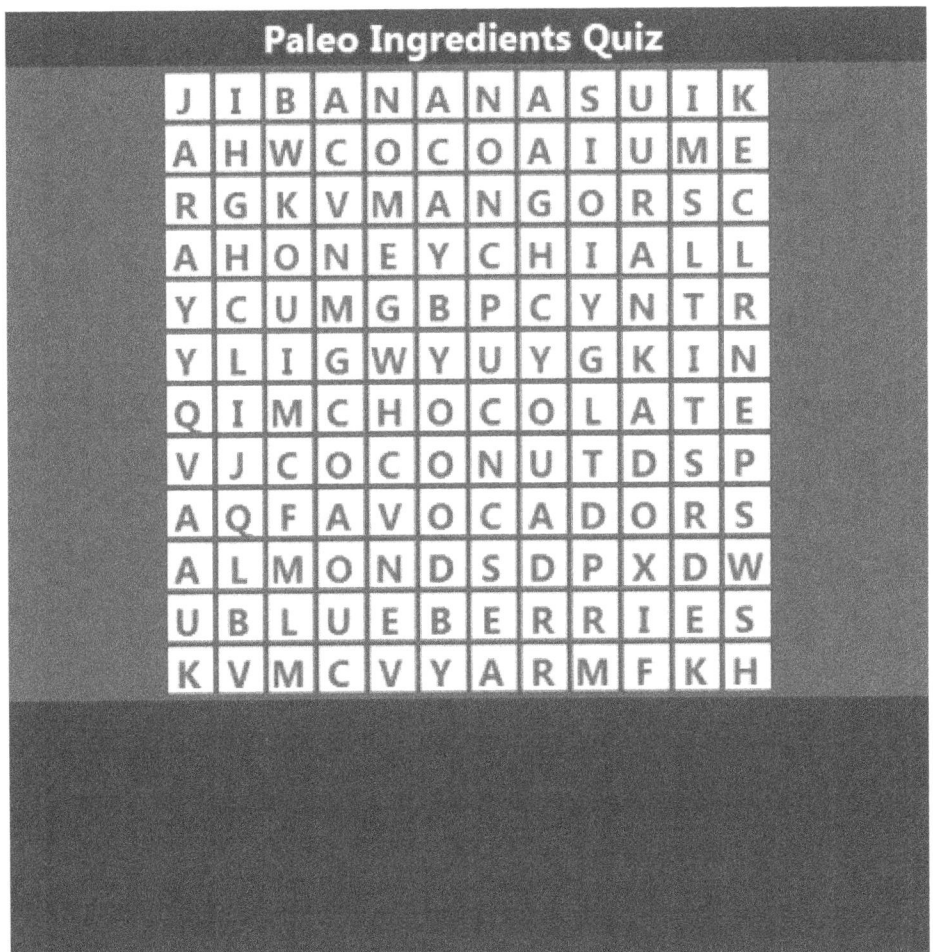

All you have to do is find 10 Paleo Ingredient related words. Use your imagination, read backwards, sideways and forward to find the correct Paleo ingredients. Go to the next page to see the correct answers!
Have fun:)

Answers

1. Chocolate
2. Coconut
3. Almonds
4. Bananas
5. Honey
6. Cocoa
7. Chia
8. Mango
9. Blueberries
10. Avocado

9 Smoothie Power Tips or The Powerful 5 Minute Smoothie Ritual

Let's talk a little bit about how you can do this even if you are a very busy person and still want to get all the healthy and powerful benefits from these delicious Paleo smoothies.

We have always loved to simplify things (usability nuts!) and like to make procedures effortless and 5 minute quick in terms of instructions and usability. Our usability tip is to use this book next to your kitchen table as you go through the preparation of your Paleo smoothies.

The following tips are most valuable if you are deciding to go on a Paleo Smoothie diet because these tips will help you get the most out of the process of making smoothies. These tips are particularly valuable if you are busy and still try to make the Paleo Smoothie Diet work for you.

9 Smoothie Power Tips or The Powerful 5 Minute Smoothie Ritual:
Be sure to pour in liquids first (it's less complicated on the whisker).

Start from the lowest speed and work up to higher speeds once the blend smoothes out. Add ice last, and use as much or as little as you'd like.

We suggest 3 cubes for each smoothie, but it is brilliantly OK to add more and make it a little slushier to attain a creamier texture. Some of our smoothies use cow's milk, or dairy free subs like almond, coconut, soy, hemp, and rice milk.

Pick your favorite, or make a mix of your own.

If you have leftover smoothie hanging in the whisker, divvy it up into an ice cube tray for simple mixing next time.

Top smoothies with fresh fruit, seeds, sliced nuts, or shredded coconut for a texture change.

Try making an oatmeal, flax seed, orange, and pineapple smoothie.

Freeze fruit for a heavier consistency.

Chop it up for simpler mixing.

Baking No Fail Muffins & Cupcakes With The Proper Baking Gear

Rule 1: Smaller Or Regular Size Is Better Than Novelty & Uniquely Shaped Size

If you have an interest in buying some silicone baking molds, or if you'd like to be better at utilizing the ones you have, keep these pointers and tricks under consideration. We have discovered that the smaller and regular sized silicone muffin molds do bake the most perfect muffins and cupcakes. If you purchase anything, we'd endorse selecting these.

If you only buy one sort of silicone baking cups, get the ordinary, cupcake-sized ones. If you are pleased to get 2 different types, we heartily advocate the minimuffin cups. Because silicone molds are so flexible and cheap, there are a large amount of specially-shaped like stars, angles, and many other forms that one can buy. While they are lovable, we suggest keeping away from them and only use the original muffin cup and cupcake cup forms because they work best.

In the name of viability, we suggest going with only 1 sizeable baking mould or a matching set made up of multiple baking molds that will accommodate a full recipe. It may be displeasing to realise this, but novelty and uniquely formed silicone baking molds are most of the time just an impulse buy. If you do finish up getting two of novelty molds, a technique to make a full recipe's worth of cake or some other bread-like concotion is to assemble a set of different baking molds, or to have additional silicone baking cups available to make little muffins or cupcakes with the batter that does not fit into your novelty formed silicone baking mould. It's sweet to have these additional nibbles available, regardless of whether they are not specifically formed, and make for fun leftover treats.

Rule 2: Grease Larger Pans

Like we mentioned silicone baking molds are additional convenient because they do not generally need greasing. Still, some baking molds, particularly the bigger ones, still need buttering, greasing and flouring. Yes, it is a bother, but it creates a difference, particularly because cakes baked in bigger silicone baking molds are at a higher chance of cracking in the elastic molds than they'd in metal pans. Flouring and greasing pans can be awe-inspiring though- one thing we do is substitute cocoa powder for flour when we are baking chocolate cakes. It makes a contribution to a better exterior appearance and is additional fun to lick out of an emptied pan.

While only bigger pans truly need greasing, it's simpler to clean smaller silicone muffin cups when they have been greased. Completely flouring and greasing these cups isn't obligatory, but you could consider spraying the molds with stain resistant cooking spray.

Alternately, you can keep them completely clean by putting paper baking cups within them and just utilising the silicone cups for structure.

Cleaning bigger silicone baking pans is pretty straightforward, but cleaning the littler ones, particularly the minimuffin cups, is tougher, particularly because there are so very many of them.

The most effective way we get round to washing these is to right away throw the empty cups into warm, soapy water, let them soak, rub the crumbs out of them, and then wash them and let them dry.

After they are dry, we may give the cups an extra wipe with a humid fabric, particularly if I have made tasty muffins in them, because they are likelier to harbour some leftover grease.

Silicone baking molds are good for more than making cakes and muffins. So do not simply make candy with your cups, but use them for all they are worth. They are perfect to serve pudding, tiramisu, creams, souflés and many other creamy desserts. We also use them to store yogurt, sauces and other liquid ingredients that we need on a daily basis. Ice creams or parfaits make a perfect match with these cute molds, too.

As well as baking both sweet treats and savoury nibbles in silicone baking cups, we suggest using them (again, typically the littler ones) for more than baking. They make great tiny serving cups for parties.

You can put tiny nibbles in them like jellybeans, nuts, and little candies, and because they come in such lovable shapes and colours, they can truly fancy-up a party platter. The additional benefit here is that, unlike the other tiny serving cups, they're washer-friendly and re-cyclable.

They also serve as internal organizers for lunchboxes and they are perfect for storing purposes.

Children just love them and this is how you can make them become interested in kitchen and baking related topics.

Rule 3: Flexibility & Be Open To More Than One Baking Supply Solution

What actually got us going on silicone baking molds wasn't an attraction to their fun shapes and bright colours, but instead the possibility of having the ability to make muffins and cupcakes in a tiny sleeping area kitchen, where we truthfully didn't have the space for a metal muffin pan.

This was a project that we did for one of our client and this is how we came up with the idea of reusable silicon molds within our own cake catering business.

The nice thing about these baking cups and molds is they stack brilliantly and take up about as much space as an espresso or coffee cup (dependent on their size). This means you can use these cups as an excuse to get shot of some of your weightier baking pans.

Having said that, we suggest clinging to your old style metal cake pans. We have both metal and silicone cake pans and apply the ones that are most practical in relation to the baking task at hand. Having available all the options is always the best way to go and we suggest using whatever is more practical for your own baking project.

When it comes down to bigger cakes, it's much better to have a stiff, more supportive material and in this case we would not recommend the more flexible silicone molds.

The one time in which we'd advocate the acquisition of a bigger silicone cake pan is if it is a specifically formed novelty pan and if you cannot find the same shape in a metal pan.

So as a general rough guide, we'd choose metal pans when handling bigger confectionary treats and use our own flexible silicon molds when it comes to smaller treats like cupcakes and muffins.

Bake Perfect Muffins & Cupcakes

Prepare the silicone cupcake molds but condition the silicone cupcake molds before their first use. Wash them in warm soapy water and wash them well. Next, coat the liners with an insubstantial layer of plant oil or nonstick spray. This strategy of "seasoning" the liners this way may simply be required for the initial few uses.

Prepare the stove and heat the stove by following the directions for the cupcake recipe. Next, adjust the rack in order that it's sitting in the middle of your oven.

Heat the cupcakes. Make the batter according to your recipe. Place a baking sheet on a level surface like a counter top or table. Position the silicone cupcake molds on the sheet. If preferred, slip into the slots of a muffin tray. Fill the silicone cupcake molds . Employing a ladle, fill the liners 2/3rds of the way with the prepared cupcake batter.

Some molds have a marked fill line.

Heat the cupcakes. Slip the cookie sheet supporting the silicone bakeware into your oven.

Check the time. When using silicone liners for the 1st time, it is crucial to watch the cupcakes meticulously, as baking times may alter a little from your ordinary cooking utensils.

Test the cupcakes to determine if they are done by inserting a toothpick or skewer into a cupcake. The cupcakes are done baking when the toothpick comes out clean.

Remove your cupcakes from the oven. Use a range mitt to hold the cookie sheet as you take them out. Be cautious. Silicone bakeware cools quick but it'll be extraordinarily hot when you first remove it.

Remove the cupcakes straight away from the molds. Once cooled, serve and enjoy your cupcakes immediately or store them.

Clean the silicone cupcake molds. Load the liners into the dishwasher or wash by hand with warm, soapy water. Given the silicone muffin molds are made from a flexible material, you can turn the silicone bakeware inside out to simply clean them.

Stack the dry and clean silicone cupcake liners within each other to store.

Always remember silicone bakeware can safely go from one intense temperature to another one, so think of utilising your liners for making frozen treats that you can put in your freezer as well as baking cupcakes.

17 Final Tips For The Paleo Lifestyle

1. Get body composition tested or retested to make quantifiable enhancements.
2. Get twenty minutes of full-on sunlight each day when practical.
3. Only eat two meals on a busy schedule or from cafes per week.
4. Commit to only buying grass-fed protein when practicable.
5. Try random fasting to work out if it's perfect for you.
6. Start bolstering with Vitamin D and Fish Oil.
7. Toss out any item in the cupboard containing sugar.
8. Write down your food consumption for one week (or even more) to help realize where you can make changes.
9. Take some time to rest and enjoy life.
10. Get off the treadmill and take your exercise sessions and running outside, or to a functional fitness gymnasium. Rather than a "cheat day", add a little indulgence like dark chocolate every day.
11. If you can include yoga and meditation into your life.
12. Get blood work tested, or retested so that you can make quantifiable changes and enhancements.
13. Eat three bigger meals each day and cut out nibbling to discover how you're feeling.
14. Try an entire thirty day Challenge to set yourself on track with the Paleo lifestyle.
15. Read a whole book about the paleo diet to teach yourself how to do it properly.
16. Check out the Resources Section in this book to educate yourself about the Paleo way of thinking and the Paleo Lifestyle

Baking Supply Secret Couponing Method

If you like to continue your path of learning more cool stuff about how to save money as you are going about your baking passions, you can do that via our interactive couponing system that you can find and download below.

You can click the link below to download our secret couponing device (just apply it to all your baking supply expenses and you are good to go!). You can use it on your computer on a daily basis in order to enjoy a life with less expenses and more baking fun!

Our interactive couponing device it totally free for you because you bought this book, and we are always adding more value and more bonuses for you because we want to give you the most valuable and usable reading and learning experience.

We are constantly throwing in new, updated, and helpful stuff into this device. We first tested it out ourselves and once we have successful results we update the device so that everyone can profit from the knowledge.

In order to get your own interactive couponing device on your own computer, you just have to download the program via the link below.

As we said above, we are constantly adding more helpful and valuable couponing tips, hacks, techniques, and ways to this program. It gets updated on a regular basis to reflect the latest trends and technologies that are available for couponing.

We will be sharing these kind of tidbits, hacks, and nuggets that will give you the results so that you can operate and enjoy your baking on a more cost effective and cost productive level!

Resources

Recipe Templates For Download & Easy Reference: http://www.chefs-resources.com/Recipe-Templates-Excel

Printable Cookbook Templates: http://office.microsoft.com/en-us/templates/recipe-cookbook-TC103462862.aspx

Top 10 Paleo Recipe Sites:

These top 10 Paleo sites are a good starting point for beginners because they offer answers to questions like what Paleo food plan should I rely on, what exactly should I eat, what is a proper Paleo breakfast, what are good bread replacements, am I allowed to eat bread and potatoes?

Once you've a Paleo beginner has adjusted his or her mindset and understod the concept of Paleo, it is really very easy to make eating the Paleo way a habit. Even the advanced users get stuck sometimes. This is the reason why we included these top 10 Paleo sites to give beginners and advanced users some unique new ideas.

These are really the best Paleo sites and resources we have been able to find so far and we use them for our own Paleo lifestyle.

http://nomnompaleo.com
http://www.paleocupboard.com
http://www.healthhomehappy.com
http://paleomg.com
http://www.healthhomehappy.com
http://eatdrinkpaleo.com.au
http://stupideasypaleo.com/recipe-index
http://www.elanaspantry.com
http://fastpaleo.com
http://www.healthhomehappy.com
http://civilizedcavemancooking.com
http://fastpaleo.com
http://www.thefoodee.com

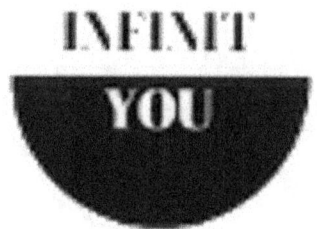

About the Publisher

InfinitYou is a hybrid general interest trade publisher. One of the first of its kind InfinitYou publishes physical books, electronic books, and audiobooks in various genres. Our publications are meant to educate, edify and entertain readers of all walks of life from babies to the elderly.

Home to more than twenty imprints such as Infinit Baby, Infinit Kids, Infinit Girl, Infinit Boy, Infinit Coloring, Infinit Swear Words, Infinit Activities, Infinit Productivity, Infinit Cat, Infinit Dog, Infinit Love, Infinit Family, Infinit Survival, Infinit Health, Infinit Beauty, Infinit Spirituality, Infinit Lifestyle, Infinit Wealth, Infinit Romance, and lots more.

www.ingramcontent.com/pod-product-compliance
Lightning Source LLC
LaVergne TN
LVHW021054100526
838202LV00083B/5876